PAST PANDEMICS AND COVID-19

by Walt K. Moon

BrightP◆int Press

San Diego, CA

BrightPoint Press

© 2021 BrightPoint Press
an imprint of ReferencePoint Press, Inc.
Printed in the United States

For more information, contact:
BrightPoint Press
PO Box 27779
San Diego, CA 92198
www.BrightPointPress.com

LIBRARY OF CONGRESS CATALOGING-IN-PUBLICATION DATA

Names: Moon, Walt K., author.
Title: Past pandemics and COVID-19 / by Walt K. Moon.
Description: San Diego, CA : BrightPoint Press, [2021] | Series: The COVID-19 pandemic |
    Includes bibliographical references and index. | Audience: Grades 7-9
Identifiers: LCCN 2020050071 (print) | LCCN 2020050072 (eBook) | ISBN 9781678200640
    (hardcover) | ISBN 9781678200657 (eBook)
Subjects: LCSH: Epidemics--Juvenile literature. | Communicable diseases--Juvenile
    literature. | COVID-19 (Disease)--Juvenile literature. | Black death--Juvenile literature. |
    Influenza--Juvenile literature.
Classification: LCC RA653.5 .M66 2021 (print) | LCC RA653.5 (eBook) | DDC 614.5/92414
    --dc23
LC record available at https://lccn.loc.gov/2020050071
LC eBook record available at https://lccn.loc.gov/2020050072

CONTENTS

- COVID-19 was first seen in China in late 2019. In early 2020, it spread across the world. The World Health Organization (WHO) declared it a pandemic on March 11, 2020.

- Pandemics are outbreaks of disease that affect a large number of people in many countries around the world. They have happened several times in history.

- The Black Death was a pandemic that struck Europe between 1347 and 1352. It involved a disease called the bubonic plague. Historians think it killed about 20 million people in Europe.

- The Spanish flu was a pandemic that happened between 1918 and 1920. It struck just as World War I (1914–1918) was ending. It involved the disease influenza. The Spanish flu killed about 50 million people worldwide.

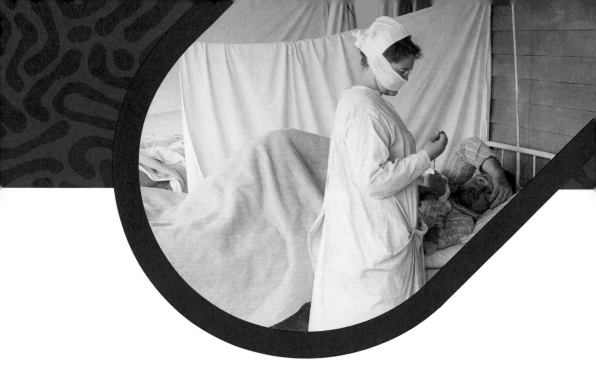

- The AIDS pandemic was recognized in the 1980s. It involves the human immunodeficiency virus (HIV). This virus leads to a condition called acquired immunodeficiency syndrome (AIDS). A person with AIDS has a weakened immune system. The AIDS pandemic has killed more than 30 million people.

- The swine flu pandemic struck in 2009. Like the Spanish flu, it involved an influenza virus. It killed about 200,000 people.

- Studying pandemics of the past can help health officials fight modern pandemics, such as COVID-19.

DECLARING A PANDEMIC

On March 11, 2020, three officials from the World Health Organization (WHO) spoke to reporters. They sat at a table with microphones. Behind them was a blue backdrop with WHO's name and logo. Video cameras captured the event.

In the center sat Dr. Tedros Adhanom Ghebreyesus. He was the director-general

Dr. Tedros Adhanom Ghebreyesus had previously served as Ethiopia's minister of health from 2005 until 2012 before becoming director-general of WHO.

of WHO. This meant he was the head of

the organization. Dr. Tedros was the first to

speak. He gave an update on COVID-19.

People had first seen the disease in Wuhan,

The city of Wuhan lies along the Yangtze River in eastern China.

China, in December 2019. In early 2020, it began spreading around the world.

Dr. Tedros began by talking about the current situation. He said, "There are now more than 118,000 cases in 114 countries,

and 4,291 people have lost their lives."[1]
He spoke about how those numbers
would soon climb higher. Then he made an
important announcement. It would change
the way the world thought about this
deadly illness. WHO was officially declaring
COVID-19 a pandemic. "Pandemic is not a
word to use lightly or carelessly," Dr. Tedros
said. "We have rung the alarm bell loud
and clear."[2]

WHAT IS A PANDEMIC?

A pandemic is a disease **outbreak**
that spreads to many countries. The
word *pandemic* comes from the ancient

Greek word *pándēmos*. *Pan* means

"all." *Demos* means "people." The word

pandemic is related to *epidemic*, which is a

smaller outbreak. Pandemics do not affect

all people in the world. But they do affect

many people across the globe.

There have been many pandemics

in human history. These diseases have

led to widespread suffering and death.

Each is unique in many ways. They have

different causes, and people responded

to them differently. But these pandemics

all share one thing in common. Each of

them changed the world. The COVID-19

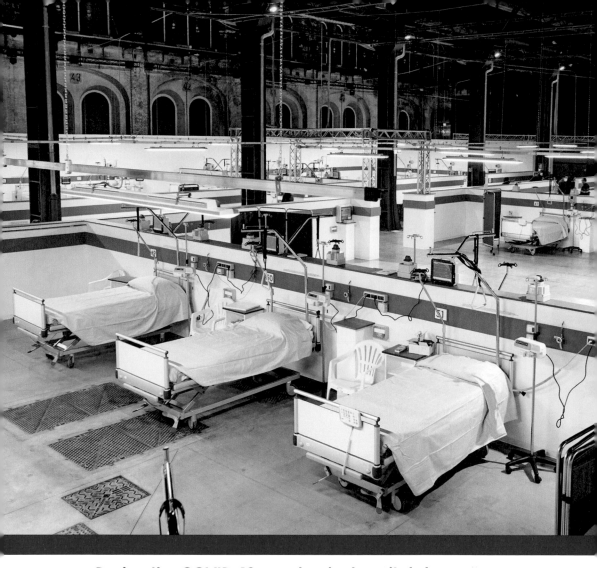

During the COVID-19 pandemic, hospitals became so full that temporary hospitals were set up in places such as large buildings.

pandemic is no different. Studying the

pandemics of the past can help people

understand more recent events.

CHAPTER ONE

WHAT WAS THE BLACK DEATH?

The Black Death was one of the worst pandemics in human history. It was a massive outbreak of a disease called the bubonic plague. This disease has struck many places at many different times. But the Black Death, which struck Europe between 1347 and 1352, was the deadliest outbreak of the disease ever.

Millions of people died during the Black Death pandemic.

Historians believe the outbreak started in central Asia. Trade routes carried it to other regions. Cases began appearing in what is now Turkey in 1347. From there it traveled to North Africa and Europe. By 1348, it was raging throughout southern Europe. And by 1349, it had reached northern Europe.

It is hard to know how many people died. There are no good **population** records from the time. But historians think up to one-third of Europeans died in the Black Death. That would total about 20 million people.

THE DISEASE

The bubonic plague is also called the plague. It is caused by a **bacterium** that mainly affects rats. Fleas spread the bacteria from rat to rat. Normally, the fleas

Black rats on ships carried the bubonic plague along trade routes.

prefer to bite rats. But if there are no rats

nearby, they will bite other mammals. That

includes humans.

Once a person is infected, the disease

begins with a fever. Parts of the body called

lymph nodes swell up. These help the

immune system, which is the body's way of fighting disease. It is normal for lymph nodes to swell when fighting an infection. But in bubonic plague, they swell so much that they are painful. Swollen lymph nodes are also known as *buboes*. This is where the disease's name comes from.

Within a few days, the person has diarrhea. He or she may become confused. Under the skin, blood vessels get clogged with bacteria. The vessels break open, and blood spills out. This forms black splotches on the skin. It can lead to blood poisoning.

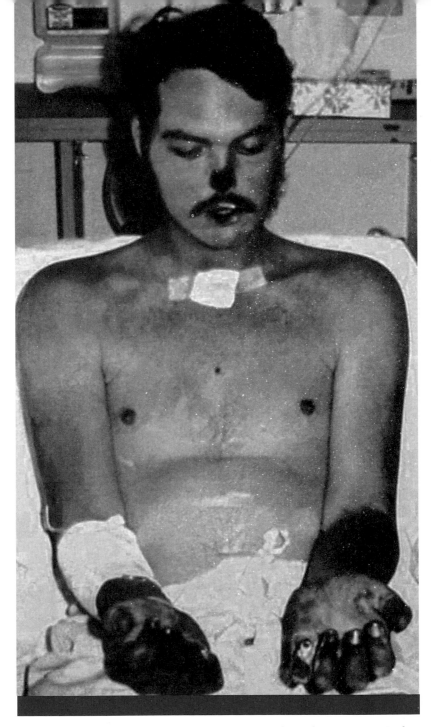

Blood clots can keep blood from flowing to certain parts of the body in a bubonic plague patient. This causes those parts to turn black and die.

And in some cases, the buboes swell so much they burst.

FIGHTING THE PLAGUE

The bubonic plague was a frightening disease. Even scarier was the fact that no one knew what caused it. The Black Death happened hundreds of years before people discovered bacteria. Some people said "bad air" caused the disease. Others blamed witches or the way the planets lined up. People even blamed religious or ethnic groups, such as the Jews. This led to terrible violence against those groups.

Costumes inspired by the clothes and masks worn by some plague doctors are popular today.

Although people didn't know what caused the disease, they took steps to fight it. They realized that it could spread from person to person. Plague doctors found sick people. They kept those people in homes or hospitals apart from others. These steps helped to slow the disease's spread. The Black Death finally faded from Europe around 1352.

The Black Death was not the first plague outbreak, and it was not the last. The world saw many major outbreaks of the plague in the next few hundred years. In the 1800s, scientists began to better understand how diseases work. In 1894, French scientist Alexandre Yersin discovered the bacterium that causes the plague. It was named *Yersinia pestis* in his honor.

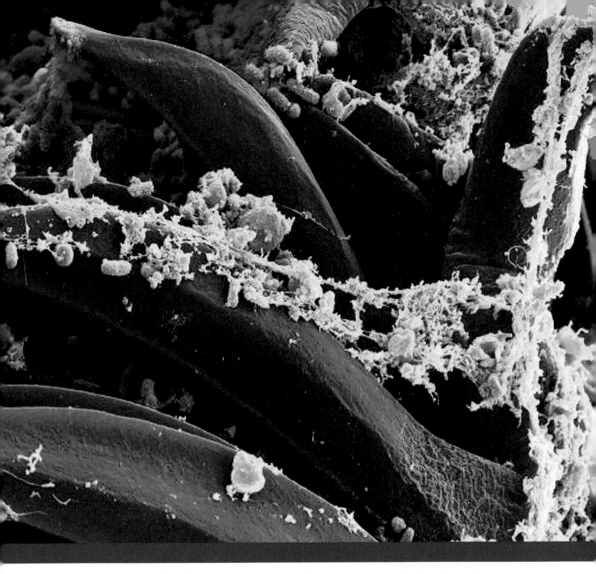

A magnified image shows Yersinia pestis *(yellow) on a flea.*

Other scientists soon realized how rats

and fleas spread the disease. People

learned that removing rats from ships and

ports could stop the plague. In the 1930s,

antibiotics let doctors treat people with the

disease. Deaths from the plague dropped

sharply, and it became rare by the 2000s.

THE BLACK DEATH AND COVID-19

COVID-19 appeared centuries after the end

of the Black Death. In that time, science

had come a long way. No one in the 1300s

knew what caused the bubonic plague.

Bacteria were not discovered until hundreds

of years later. By contrast, people quickly

learned much about COVID-19.

A virus called SARS-CoV-2 causes

COVID-19. A lab in China started decoding

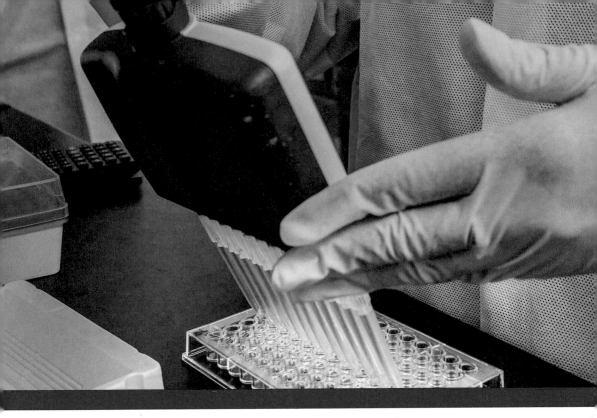

Finding the full genome of SARS-CoV-2 allowed scientists to make a test that could determine who was infected with the virus.

the virus's genome in late December

2019. This is the **genetic** code inside

the virus that makes it work the way it

does. By January 2, the scientists had

the full genome. Another lab decoded the

full genome on January 5. Decoding the

virus's genome let scientists compare it to other known viruses. It also helped them figure out how to treat the disease. This gave them a head start in understanding COVID-19.

Professor Zhang Yongzhen was one of the scientists studying the genome. He said, "It took us less than 40 hours, so very, very

QUARANTINE

The word *quarantine* means to stay apart from other people to stop spreading disease. The word comes from the time of the Black Death. Ships coming to Venice, Italy, had to wait offshore for forty days before coming to shore. *Quarantine* comes from the Italian word for forty.

fast. Then I realized that this virus is closely related to SARS, probably 80 percent." An outbreak of the respiratory disease SARS, or severe acute respiratory syndrome, struck China in 2003. "So certainly, it was very dangerous," Zhang said.[3]

The scientific responses to the Black Death and COVID-19 were very different. But the pandemics do have some things in common. Both spread through human travel. The Black Death began in central Asia. It then spread to Europe through trading routes. Infected fleas and rats hitched rides with these traders. With

COVID-19, widespread airplane travel helped it spread across the world quickly.

The idea of **isolation** was important in both pandemics. People in the 1300s knew the plague could spread between people. Workers called plague doctors helped sick people. They kept people apart to slow the spread. People stayed in their homes or in plague hospitals.

COVID-19 can also spread from person to person. People followed social distancing rules to stay healthy. Health officials told them to stay at least 6 feet (1.8 m) apart. They also recommended people stay home as much as possible. Stadiums, restaurants, schools, and businesses closed. All these actions were meant to slow the spread of COVID-19.

PLAGUE PPE

Modern doctors wear personal protective equipment (PPE) when helping COVID-19 patients. This may include a gown, gloves, and a face mask. Plague doctors during outbreaks in the 1600s also had special gear. The most famous part was a large mask shaped like a bird's beak. The beak contained a mix of herbs. The idea was that poisoned air caused the disease. The herbs were supposed to protect the plague doctor. But in reality, this did not work.

CHAPTER TWO

WHAT WAS THE SPANISH FLU?

In 1918, the world was at war. Millions of people had died in World War I (1914–1918). But as the war was ending, a pandemic was beginning. The disease known as the Spanish flu would take even more lives than the devastating war.

The Spanish flu was caused by the influenza virus. This virus affects the

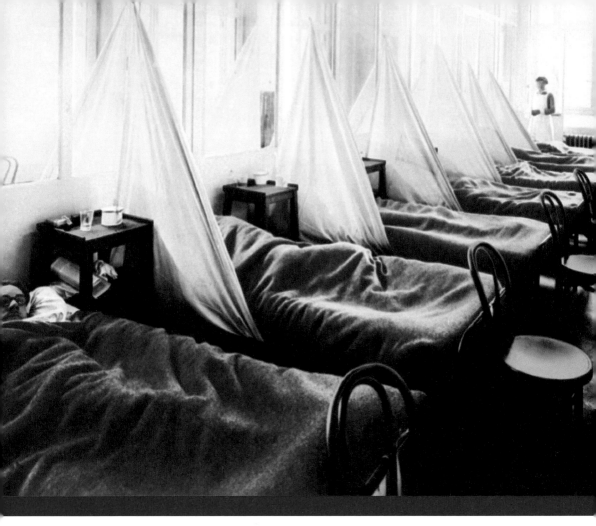

Hospitals filled with patients during the Spanish flu outbreak.

respiratory system. It causes symptoms

such as chills and fever. In severe cases, the

symptoms are worse. The lungs can fill with

fluid. This can be deadly.

Different types of influenza virus cause different kinds of flu. The flu is a common disease. People get it every year. This is called seasonal flu. Today it kills thousands of people each year. But it rarely becomes a pandemic. In 1918, a new **strain** of

NAMING THE FLU

During World War I, most countries in Europe were fighting. They did not allow coverage of the pandemic in newspapers. They didn't want to panic their people. But Spain was not involved in the war. It didn't block stories about the flu. People only saw stories from Spain about the pandemic. They thought it started in Spain. This is why it became known as the Spanish flu. No one knows for sure where it really started.

influenza appeared. It could spread quickly. It was also more dangerous than the seasonal flu. Unlike common flu strains, it killed people who were young and otherwise healthy. This combination led to a pandemic.

THE SPREAD

One of the first outbreaks happened in Kansas in March 1918. The disease appeared at a military camp. It then spread across the United States in the spring. This first wave of Spanish flu was not severe. Many people got sick, but deaths were not unusually high.

The first known cases of the Spanish flu were in soldiers.

In the fall of 1918, a second wave reached its peak. The disease became more dangerous. People died within days or even hours of showing symptoms. Their lungs filled with fluid, killing them. Scientists are not certain what made the second wave deadlier. One common theory blames mutations, or changes to the virus over time. Another points to troop movements during World War I, which caused the virus to spread quickly.

The pandemic faded in 1920. By that time, about 675,000 people in the United States had died. Worldwide, the total was about 50 million. An estimated 500 million people had been infected. That was roughly one-third of the world's population.

CONTROLLING THE PANDEMIC

By the early 1900s, scientists knew far more about diseases than they did during the Black Death. They understood that a tiny **microbe** caused the flu. Still, there were gaps in their knowledge. They knew little about viruses. No one would see a virus until the 1930s. Microscopes were not advanced enough until then. Vaccines existed for some diseases. But there were none for the flu.

Experts realized that whatever kind of microbe caused the flu, it spread through the air. They knew that droplets from coughing and sneezing could infect people. The American Public Health Association (APHA) wrote a report about the pandemic. It said the disease was "spread solely by

Some people gargled with salt water to try to prevent the Spanish flu.

discharges from the nose and throats

of infected persons."[4] Health officials

took steps to stop that kind of spread

from happening.

During the Spanish flu pandemic, people sprayed their throats with a liquid that was thought to stop the growth of the microbes causing the disease.

One of those steps was closing public gathering places. The APHA recommended closing bars, dance halls, and movie theaters. It said churches could stay open, but services should be quick. It recommended avoiding streetcars.

They were often crowded, and there was little fresh air. Health officials recommended that people walk to work instead.

Different cities had different death rates from the flu. Modern experts have studied why. They found that cities that quickly made public health restrictions did better. In papers from 2007, experts made a notable comparison. Saint Louis, Missouri, acted two days after reporting its first cases. Philadelphia, Pennsylvania, waited more than two weeks. The death rate in Philadelphia was up to eight times higher than that of Saint Louis. Dr. Anthony

Fauci was the director of the National Institute of Allergy and Infectious Diseases (NIAID). He said, "These important papers suggest that a primary lesson of the 1918 influenza pandemic is that it is critical to intervene early."[5]

Another step people took was wearing face masks. These would stop droplets from leaving the mouth. Masks were usually made of a material called gauze. This material is a fabric often used to cover wounds. To use it as a mask, people would fold the gauze into a triangular shape. It would cover up the mouth and nose.

People wore masks to try to stop the spread of the Spanish flu.

Some cities made rules about mask wearing. In the fall of 1918, San Francisco, California, required masks in public places. The penalty was a fine of up to ten dollars. People could also be jailed for ten days. Similar rules were passed in San Diego, California, and other cities.

THE SPANISH FLU AND COVID-19

The Spanish flu and COVID-19 both

spread around the world. But COVID-19

spread more quickly. Olga Jonas works

at the Harvard Global Health Institute.

An interviewer asked her to compare

ANTI-MASK GROUPS

Some people opposed mask rules during
the Spanish flu pandemic. A group called the
Anti-Mask League formed in San Francisco.
In 2020 the science was clear. Masks helped
slow the spread of COVID-19. But some people
still opposed mask requirements. In both
pandemics, people against masks said they
didn't want the government telling them what
to do.

the two pandemics. She explained that transportation technology made a big difference. She said, "In 1918, there was no air travel. People move around much more, and the spread of a virus is much faster than before, when people traveled by ship or horse, or didn't travel much at all."[6]

The Spanish flu was an unusual flu. It killed many young, healthy people. COVID-19 was different. It was most severe in older people and in those with other health problems. It did sicken and kill young people. But this was less common.

The two pandemics do share things in common. Both were caused by viruses. For the Spanish flu, it was an influenza virus. For COVID-19, it was a coronavirus. These are different kinds of viruses, but they work in similar ways. A virus takes over a living cell. It makes the cell produce copies of the virus. The cell then dies. The virus spreads to other cells in the body. This makes a person sick.

The way health officials responded to the pandemics was also similar. Both diseases spread through droplets. Staying away from others, closing public spaces, and wearing

People wore masks during the COVID-19 pandemic just like they did during the Spanish flu.

masks were all used in 1918. They were

used in 2020 too.

During the Spanish flu pandemic, soldiers

at military camps had to eat 5 feet (1.5 m)

apart. During the COVID-19 pandemic,

health officials recommended staying

6 feet (1.8 m) apart in public. This is known

as social distancing. It is sometimes called

physical distancing.

Schools across the United States

closed during the COVID-19 pandemic.

PANDEMICS AND PRESIDENTS

Woodrow Wilson was the US president during the Spanish flu pandemic. He caught the flu in April 1919. Wilson was in Paris, France, for peace talks after World War I. The government kept his illness secret. Private letters from his doctor revealed the truth decades later. In October 2020, President Donald Trump tested positive for COVID-19. He announced this on Twitter. Trump went to the hospital for a few days. He recovered from the disease and returned to work the next week.

Students learned online in the spring of 2020. Some returned to classrooms in the fall. Others continued to take classes online. During the flu pandemic, online learning was not an option. Schools were not widely closed in the United States. Other countries had different school policies. The United Kingdom closed elementary schools. France made sick children and their siblings stay home from school.

CHAPTER THREE

WHAT IS THE AIDS PANDEMIC?

n 1981, doctors noticed several cases of a rare lung infection in Los Angeles, California. They also saw an unusual form of cancer. These health problems were affecting young, healthy, gay men. The cause seemed to be a problem with the immune system. Scientists worked to figure

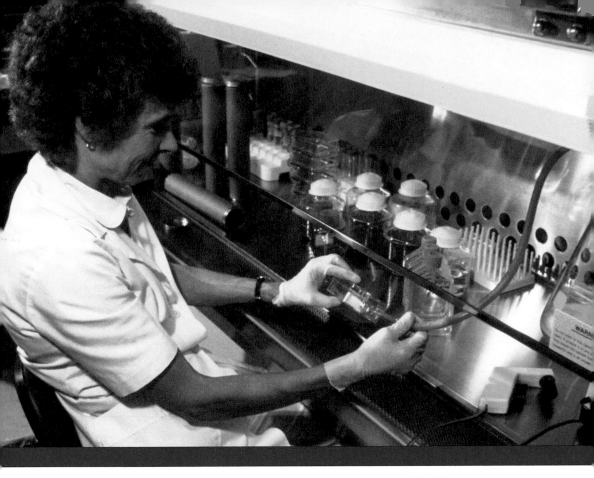

Scientists studied AIDS in the 1980s to try to figure out how to treat it.

out what was going on. They soon found

that the problems also affected drug users

who shared needles.

The next year, scientists named the

disease AIDS. This stands for acquired

immunodeficiency syndrome. AIDS results

in a weakened immune system. This

leaves the body vulnerable to infections

and diseases.

In the mid-1980s, scientists discovered

the virus that causes AIDS. And in 1986,

they gave this virus an official name: HIV.

This stands for human immunodeficiency

DR. ANTHONY FAUCI

In 1984, Dr. Anthony Fauci became the head of the NIAID. He helped lead the fight against AIDS. In 2020, he had the same job. He helped lead the fight against the COVID-19 pandemic. Dr. Fauci was named to the White House Coronavirus Task Force. He often appeared at press briefings alongside President Trump.

virus. By this time, HIV/AIDS was a worldwide problem. By the end of 1986, it had spread to eighty-five countries. There were more than 38,000 cases in all.

The numbers grew dramatically as the pandemic continued. By the year 2000, about 33 million people were living with HIV. About 14 million people had died from AIDS. By 2020, the death toll had risen to about 32.7 million. No end to the pandemic was in sight.

SPREAD AND TREATMENT

HIV often spreads through unprotected sex. It can also spread through shared needles.

Sometimes HIV transfers from mother to child, but there are treatments that can reduce the risk.

The key is bodily fluids. The virus spreads

from person to person through these

fluids. This is a reason why early cases

were seen in gay men and drug users.

The virus spreads especially easily when

men have sex with men. But it can spread

during other kinds of sexual activity too. Researchers also learned that it can spread from mothers to children during or after pregnancy.

A person infected with HIV does not automatically have AIDS. One of two things must happen for AIDS to be diagnosed. The number of immune cells in the person's blood must drop below a certain level. Or the person must get an infection that is common in those with weakened immune systems.

There is no cure for HIV/AIDS, and the immune system cannot stop it.

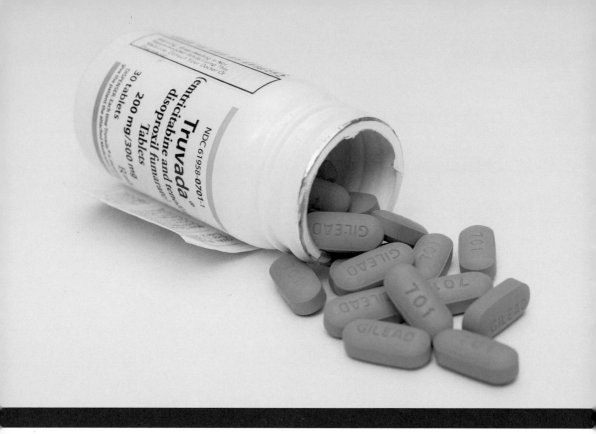

Certain drugs can reduce the risk of getting HIV if exposed.

Without treatment, a person with AIDS can

survive for about three years. However,

treatment has come a long way. Medication

can stop HIV from progressing to AIDS

in the first place. People without HIV can

also take medications that can prevent

them from becoming infected with it if they are exposed.

HIV/AIDS AND COVID-19

Dr. David Ho is an HIV/AIDS researcher. He began studying the disease in the early 1980s. Dr. Ho's work helped lead to modern treatments for AIDS. In 2020, he was interviewed about how the AIDS pandemic compared to COVID-19. He noted several similarities.

Dr. Ho explained that in both pandemics, doctors scrambled to find treatments. They tried using drugs that were created for other purposes. These treatments were mostly ineffective. But doctors were trying to help in any way they could. He said, "I would say there were at least 3–4 dozen drugs that were put forward as potential treatments or cures for HIV; none of that panned out. . . . [With COVID-19], we went through the same."[7]

COVID-19 DISRUPTION

HIV medicines help millions of people around the world. The COVID-19 pandemic threatened those treatments. Countries closed businesses and borders to slow the spread of the virus. But this also made it harder to make and distribute HIV medicines, especially in poorer countries. Researchers estimated that a six-month disruption could lead to 500,000 more deaths from AIDS.

Dr. Ho also noted that with both diseases, patients often died alone. With AIDS, this was due to **stigma**. People often discriminated against gay people, and many patients were gay. Dr. Ho said that early HIV patients "were shunned by friends and family."[8] People were also afraid of the disease. Science showed that AIDS could not be spread to others nearby. But people still stayed away from those with the disease.

With COVID-19, patients also died alone. However, it was not due to stigma. The disease could spread easily from person to person. Simply breathing nearby could infect others. People had to stay away for their own safety. Families had to say goodbye to loved ones over video chats. Many people faced this difficult situation.

The pandemics were different in some ways. HIV/AIDS is a chronic condition. This means that it lasts for life. The immune system cannot defeat the virus. COVID-19 is an acute condition. That means it lasts for a limited time. If it does not kill the patient, the immune system eventually defeats the virus. The person gets better. Although the COVID-19 infection is acute, scientists

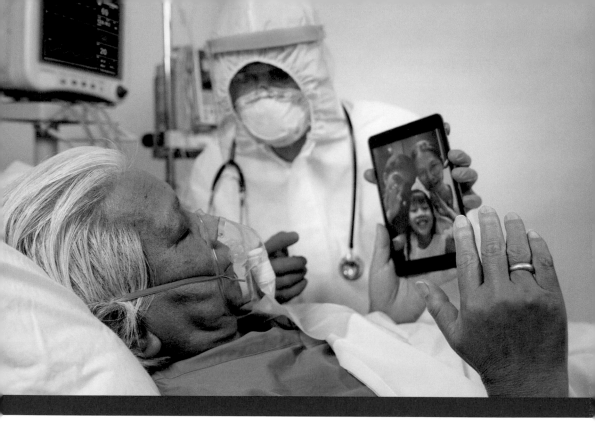

Families of COVID-19 patients could not visit their loved ones in person.

were still learning about the disease's

long-term effects in 2020. For example, they

found evidence that the virus may cause

permanent heart damage. More research

was needed on this and other possible

long-term effects.

CHAPTER FOUR

WHAT IS THE SWINE FLU?

The Spanish flu was not the last influenza pandemic. Two more struck in the 1900s, one in 1957 and one in 1968. Another happened in 2009. It became known as the swine flu pandemic. This name came from the fact that similar viruses had been seen in pigs. It was also called H1N1, which refers to the type of influenza

The swine flu got its name because it started in pigs. These animals are sometimes called swine.

virus involved. The Spanish flu virus was the

same type, though the two viruses were not

closely related.

The first US cases of swine flu appeared

in April 2009. A child in California was

diagnosed on April 15. Soon after, another

child living 130 miles (210 km) away was

diagnosed. The two kids had not been in

contact. This showed that the virus was

already spreading through communities. It

was a type of flu that had never been seen

in humans before.

NAMING INFLUENZA VIRUSES

There are four kinds of influenza viruses.
They are called A, B, C, and D. The A viruses
are further divided into many different types.
They are named for two proteins on the viruses,
which are known as H and N for short. The
different H and N proteins are numbered.
The 2009 swine flu was A(H1N1). So was the
Spanish flu. One seasonal flu is A(H3N2).
The 1957 flu pandemic was A(H2N2).

The symptoms of swine flu are like those of other flus. They include fever, coughing, a sore throat, a runny nose, and aches. Most people recovered from swine flu. But for some, the disease became more severe. In normal flus, the majority of deaths happen among those over sixty-five. But with swine flu, most of those who died were under sixty-five. Those with health conditions such as heart disease, lung disease, and **asthma** faced higher risks. These are the same groups that face the most danger from seasonal flu.

The swine flu caused a runny nose and chills, similar to other flus. But it affected some people much worse than others.

THE VIRUS SPREADS

The Centers for Disease Control and

Prevention (CDC) is a US public health

agency. It went to work right away. By

April 21, 2009, it had started working on a

vaccine. And by April 24, it had decoded

the virus's genome. The CDC shared the

genome with international researchers.

The virus continued to spread through

the spring. On June 11, WHO declared the

swine flu a pandemic. Dr. Margaret Chan

was the director-general of WHO at the

time. She said, "No previous pandemic

has been detected so early or watched

so closely. . . . We have a head start. This places us in a strong position."[9] By this time, more than seventy countries had reported cases.

On June 25, the CDC estimated that the number of cases in the US had reached 1 million. By September, the US government had approved four vaccines for the virus. The next year, WHO declared the pandemic over. It lasted about sixteen months. During that time, scientists estimated that about 24 percent of the world's population was infected. About 200,000 people died.

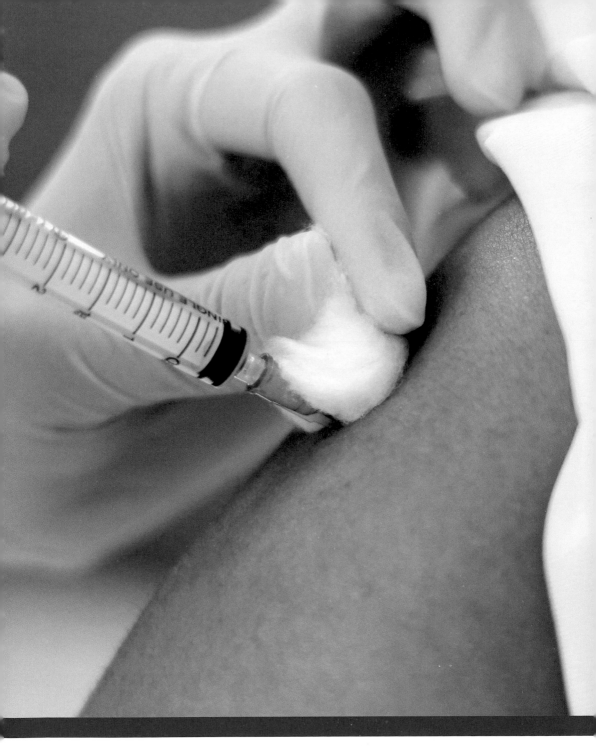

The swine flu vaccine helped prevent people from getting sick from the virus.

THE SWINE FLU AND COVID-19

The swine flu and COVID-19 pandemics both happened in the age of modern medicine. Scientists knew a lot about diseases and how to fight them. With swine flu, scientists were already familiar with other influenza viruses. And with COVID-19, they were already familiar with other coronaviruses. Scientists decoded the genomes of both viruses just days after discovering them. This helped them understand how the viruses worked.

One key difference between the pandemics was testing. Testing people for a virus is an important part of fighting a disease. It helps health officials know how the virus is spreading. In 2009, most states already had labs that could test for the swine flu. But with COVID-19, testing had major challenges. There were no existing tests for the virus. The CDC sent out testing

SOCIAL MEDIA IN A PANDEMIC

People were using social media in 2009. Facebook and Twitter existed. But by 2020, social media was far more popular. People used it to spread information and medical advice. But they also spread false information about COVID-19. Misinformation can make it harder to fight a pandemic.

kits to US labs on February 5. But many of these kits didn't work.

Experts said testing problems gave the virus a chance to spread. Dr. Tedros of WHO said, "You cannot fight a fire blindfolded. And we cannot stop this pandemic if we don't know who is infected."[10]

Another difference was in making a vaccine. In 2009, scientists were already familiar with influenza vaccines. Vaccines for seasonal flu are created each year. Vaccine research for the swine flu started in April. In October, more than 20 million doses were

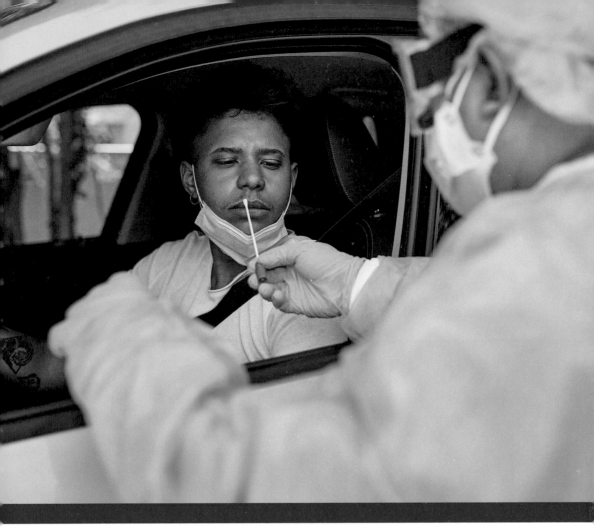

Most COVID-19 tests required taking a nasal swab.

available. This was fewer than the CDC had

hoped to make. But many Americans were

able to get a vaccine just six months after

the disease appeared.

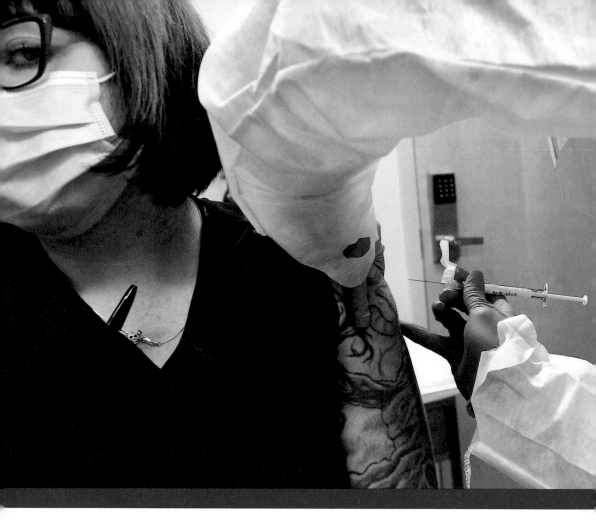

Some people volunteered to participate in COVID-19 vaccine trials in 2020. The trials helped scientists learn if their vaccines were effective.

The situation with COVID-19 was different. No vaccines against coronaviruses had ever been approved before. Some research had been done on earlier viruses.

But there was never a pressing demand for a vaccine. Now, COVID-19 created an urgent need. Scientists worked quickly to create a vaccine. This kind of project usually takes years to complete. By the fall of 2020, several vaccines were in the late stages of testing. Two had been submitted to the US Food and Drug Administration for approval by the end of November. Researchers hoped to get a vaccine approved and distributed in 2021.

HISTORY INFORMING THE PRESENT

The COVID-19 pandemic shocked many people around the world. It spread rapidly.

PANDEMIC DEATHS

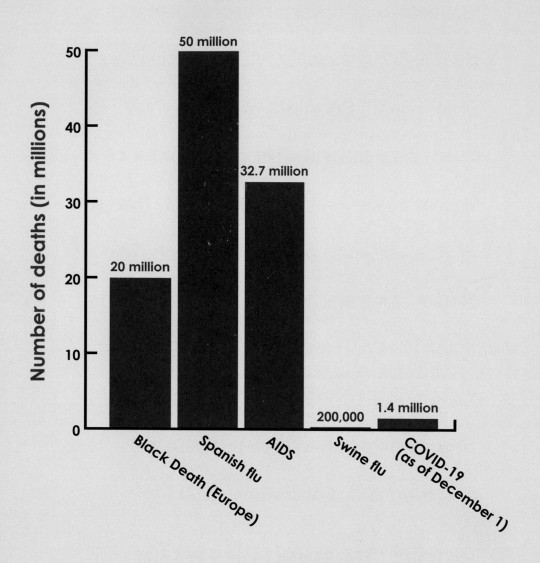

This graph shows the global deaths for several pandemics, except for the Black Death, which includes deaths in Europe only.

Businesses, schools, and public places closed. Many people lost their jobs. Others began working from home when offices closed. Everyday life changed for people across the globe. By December 1, 2020, the disease had killed more than 1.4 million people worldwide.

But disease experts were ready. They had studied the pandemics of the past. They learned important lessons. Scientists, doctors, and health officials used these lessons to fight the COVID-19 pandemic.

GLOSSARY

asthma

a disease that causes trouble with breathing

bacterium

a tiny, one-celled living thing that may cause disease

genetic

related to the material inside living cells that lets them pass traits to their offspring

isolation

the practice of separating sick people from others in order to prevent the spread of a disease

microbe

a living thing too small to see with the naked eye

outbreak

the rapid spread of a disease

population

the total number of people living in a particular area

stigma

shame that is often the result of unfair treatment

strain

a specific type of a virus or bacterium

SOURCE NOTES

INTRODUCTION: DECLARING A PANDEMIC

1. "WHO Director-General's Opening Remarks at the Media Briefing on COVID-19 – 11 March 2020," *World Health Organization*, March 11, 2020. www.who.int.

2. "WHO Director-General's Opening Remarks."

CHAPTER ONE: WHAT WAS THE BLACK DEATH?

3. Quoted in Charlie Campbell, "Exclusive: The Chinese Scientist Who Sequenced the First COVID-19 Genome Speaks Out," *Time*, August 24, 2020. https://time.com.

CHAPTER TWO: WHAT WAS THE SPANISH FLU?

4. Quoted in "The Public Health Response," *Human Virology at Stanford*, n.d. http://virus.stanford.edu.

5. Quoted in "Rapid Response Was Crucial to Containing the 1918 Flu Pandemic," *National Institutes of Health*, April 2, 2007. www.nih.gov.

6. Quoted in Liz Mineo, "Harvard Expert Compares 1918 Flu, COVID-19," *Harvard Gazette*, May 19, 2020. https://news.harvard.edu.

CHAPTER THREE: WHAT IS THE AIDS PANDEMIC?

7. Quoted in Kevin Kunzmann, "What COVID-19 Shares with SARS, Influenza, HIV," *Contagion Live*, August 11, 2020. www.contagionlive.com.

8. Quoted in Kunzmann, "What COVID-19 Shares."

CHAPTER FOUR: WHAT IS THE SWINE FLU?

9. "World Now at the Start of 2009 Influenza Pandemic," *World Health Organization*, June 11, 2009. www.who.int.

10. "WHO Director-General's Opening Remarks at the Media Briefing on COVID-19 – 16 March 2020," *World Health Organization*, March 16, 2020. www.who.int.

FOR FURTHER RESEARCH

BOOKS

Barbara Krasner, *Bubonic Plague: How the Black Death Changed History*. North Mankato, MN: Capstone, 2019.

Barbara Krasner, *Influenza: How the Flu Changed History*. North Mankato, MN: Capstone, 2019.

Martha London, *The Spread of COVID-19*. Minneapolis, MN: Abdo, 2020.

INTERNET SOURCES

"Black Death," *DK Find Out!*, n.d. www.dkfindout.com.

"The History of Pandemics," *Time for Kids*, May 18, 2020. www.timeforkids.com.

"UTHSC Coronavirus Facts for Kids," *University of Tennessee Health Science Center*, n.d. https://uthsc.edu.

WEBSITES

CDC Past Pandemics
www.cdc.gov/flu/pandemic-resources/basics/past
-pandemics.html

The Centers for Disease Control and Prevention (CDC) Past Pandemics page provides information on several past pandemics to hit the world.

Ready.gov: Pandemic
www.ready.gov/pandemic

This US government website includes information about how to prepare for a pandemic.

World Health Organization
www.who.int

The World Health Organization (WHO) provides global health information and guidelines on a variety of topics, including COVID-19.

INDEX

IMAGE CREDITS

ABOUT THE AUTHOR

Walt K. Moon is a writer who lives in Minnesota. He enjoys learning and reading about all kinds of science, including the science of public health.